OVERSIZE

D1475480

Beauty & Healthcare

PACKAGE DESIGN

Beauty and Healthcare Package Design

PIE BOOKS

2-32-4, Minami-Otsuka, Toshima-ku, Tokyo 170-0005 JAPAN

Tel : +81-3-5395-4811 Fax : +81-3-5395-4812

e-mail :

editor@piebooks.com

sales@piebooks.com

http://www.piebooks.com

ISBN978-89444-729-5 C3070

Printed in Japan

Contents

"Organic" and "sweets" are the new keywords

This book contains a special collection of packaging and bottle design samples from health and beauty products ranging from cosmetics to perfume, body care, hair care and bath products as well as nutritional supplements. The vast majority of the packaging is for products that are marketed to women and adjectives such as "cute," "fashionable" and "cool" are appropriate for any one of them. As we searched the stores, on the Internet and in magazines etc for packaging samples to include in this book, we discovered that the words "sweets" and "organic" were in frequent use.

The word "organic," when defined in simple terms, describes a product that does not contain chemicals and to the greatest possible extent uses ingredients that are sourced from nature. As a means of expressing the content of such products, their packaging is often designed using earth tones and images from nature such as fruits, plants, the sea and the sky. Florame on page 118 and IKOVE on page 121 are examples of this approach. The customer receives the powerful message from the packaging design that nature equates to peace of mind and a sense of security.

With the "sweets" approach, packaging and perfume are made to resemble cakes and desserts. The SEXY GIRL hand and body cream on page 40 comes in fruit punch, strawberry mille feuille and peach tart fragrances and the packaging incorporates visuals of mouth-watering sweets for each fragrance. The packaging for the Bourjois face powder on page 52 resembles a bar of chocolate. Incorporating the "sweets" concept, so popular among young women, into the products that are marketed to women has become a successful ploy in stimulating discussion among and attracting the attention of female consumers.

We hope that designers not only in the packaging and product design industry but also in other creative fields find this book useful as a source of creative ideas for design to "capture the female heart."

Finally, we would like to take this opportunity to express our sincere appreciation to all the public relations and advertising staff and creators who took the time to provide us with such splendid material for the book.

Pie Books, Editorial Department

はじめに

キーワードは「オーガニック」と「スイーツ」。

本書は、化粧品から香水・ボディケア・ヘアケア・入浴剤・サプリメントまで美容と健康に関する商品のパッケージやボトルのデザインを特集しています。

やはりこの分野は、女性をターゲットとしている商品のパッケージが圧倒的に多く、「かわいい」「おしゃれ」「かっこいい」といった形容詞がどの作品にも当てはまります。

また、今回、掲載作品を店頭や Web、雑誌などでさがしていくなかで、トレンドとして頻繁に目にした言葉が「オーガニック」と「スイーツ」でした。

「オーガニック」は、簡単に言うと製品の成分に化学成分を使っていないもの、なるべく天然由来の成分を使用したものです。そうした製品のパッケージは、やはり内容を表すような、アースカラーの色使いであったり、果物や植物、海や空といった自然をモチーフにデザインされたものが多く見られます。例えば、118 ページの 'Florame' や、121 ページの 'IKOVE' などです。パッケージのデザインからも「天然＝安心・安全」といった印象を強く受けます。

もうひとつの「スイーツ」は、パッケージや香りを、お菓子やデザートに似せたものです。40 ページの 'SEXY GIRL' のハンド & ボディクリームは「フルーツパンチ」「ストロベリーミルフィーユ」「ピーチタルト」の香りがあり、パッケージにもそれぞれ、おい

しそうなスイーツのビジュアルがデザインされています。また、52ページの'BOURJOIS'のフェイスパウダーは板チョコにそっくりなパッケージです。女性をターゲットにした商品に、女性が大好きな「スイーツ」を取り込みこみ、話題や注目を集めること成功しています。

上記の作品を初め、本書が「女性の心を掴むデザイン」のアイデアソースとして、パッケージやプロダクトデザインに携わる方はもとより、様々なクリエイターの方々の参考となれば幸いです。

最後になりましたが、お忙しいなか、本書の制作にあたり、素晴らしい作品をご提供くださった各社広報・宣伝部門の方々、クリエイターの皆様にこの場を借りて、心より御礼申し上げます。

ピエ・ブックス　編集部

クレジットは、ブランド名、国名、スタッフクレジットの順に掲載をしています。
Credit order: Brand name, County name, Production staff.

●制作スタッフクレジットの制作者呼称は以下のように省略して記載しています。
The following abbreviations are used in for production staff names :

CL：Client　クライアント
CD：Creative Director　クリエイティブディレクター
AD：Art Director　アートディレクター
D：Designer　デザイナー
P：Photographer　フォトグラファー
I：Illustrator　イラストレーター
CW：Copywriter　コピーライター
DF：Desgn Firm　デザイン事務所
SB：Submittor　出品者

●上記以外の制作者呼称は、省略せずに記載しています。
Full names of all others involved in the creation/production of the work.

●提供者の希望によりクレジットデータの一部を記載していないものがあります。
Please note that some credit data has been omitted at the request of the submittor.

本書は、デザイン性の高い製品を弊社の独自の基準で選び掲載しています。製品の内容、効用、価格などを紹介する本ではありません。あらかじめご了承ください。
The works presented in this book were selected for their design qualities by our editorial staff based on our own criteria.
Please be aware that this book does not provide product-related information including content, benefits or price.

また、掲載作品に関しては、すでに製造・販売をしていないもの、デザイン・内容が現行のものと異なるものも含まれます。また、今後、予告なく変更、製造・販売を中止するものも含まれます。あらかじめご了承ください。
Please be aware that this book may feature product packaging for products that are no longer being manufactured or sold or differ in terms of design and content from the current version of the packaging. Also featured is packaging for products that may change without notice, or for which manufacturing may be discontinued or be removed from sale.

掲載作品は、なるべくブランドごとに紹介をしたいという編集意図により、「スキンケア」「メイクアップ」「フレグランス」「ヘアケア」「バス用品」「サプリメント、その他」の6つのコンテンツのいずれか1つのコンテンツで、まとめて紹介をしている場合があります。そのため、製品本来の使用目的、メーカーの販売意図とは異なるコンテンツで紹介をされているものもあります。あらかじめご了承ください。
The editorial decision to profile as much as possible the material in the book according to brand may result in some material being profiled in any one of the six categories, namely skin care, makeup, fragrance, hair care, bath products, and nutritional supplements etc. Please be aware that some products therefore may be profiled without reference to the product's original purpose of use or the manufacturer's aim in marketing the product.

Skin-care

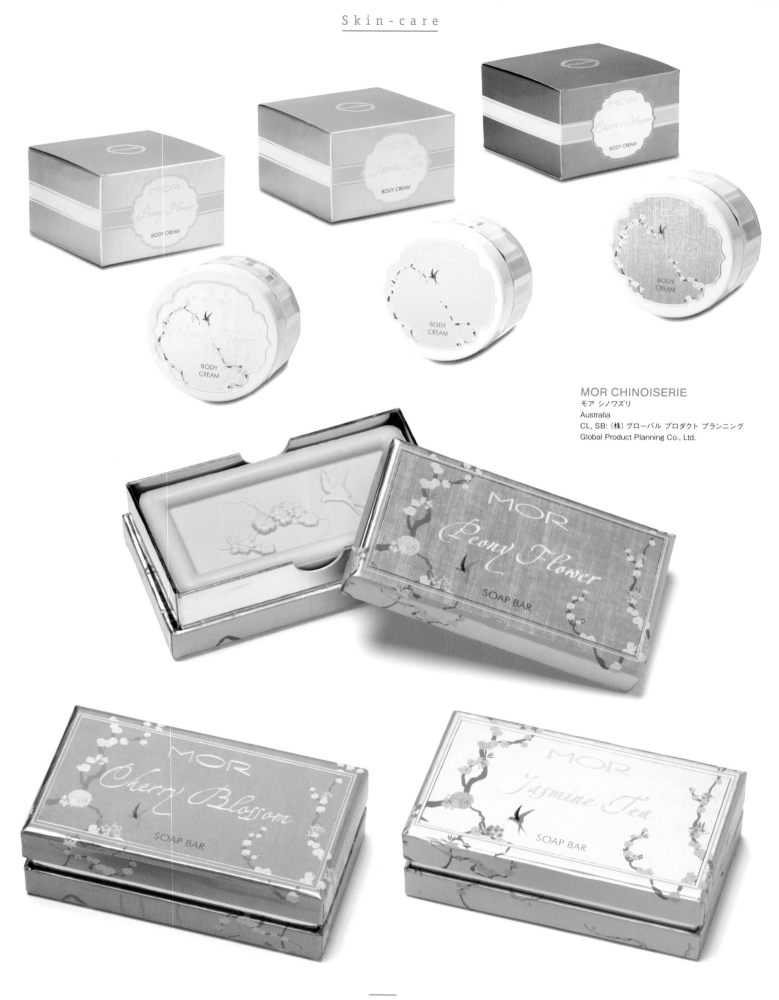

MOR CHINOISERIE
モア シノワズリ
Australia
CL, SB:（株）グローバル プロダクト プランニング
Global Product Planning Co., Ltd.

MOR
Peony Lip Silk
MOR
Peony
Lip Silk

MOR
Jasmine Lip Silk
MOR
Jasmine
Lip Silk

MOR
Cherry Lip Silk
MOR
Cherry
Lip Silk

MOR
Jasmine
Lip Silk

MOR CHINOISERIE
モア シノワズリ
Australia
CL, SB: ㈱ グローバル プロダクト プランニング
Global Product Planning Co., Ltd.

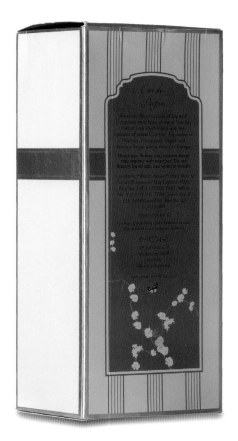

  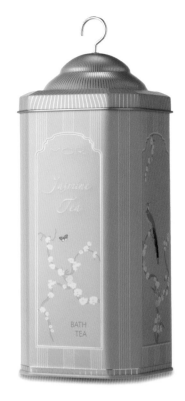

MOR EMPOIUM
モア エンポリアム
Australia
CL, SB:（株）グローバル プロダクト プランニング
Global Product Planning Co., Ltd.

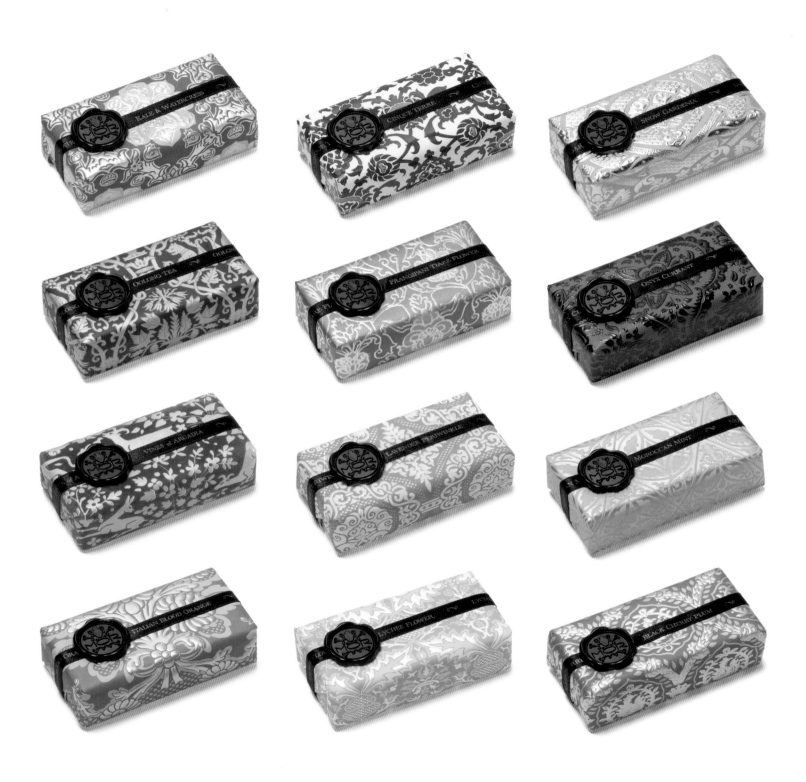

Kathleen Lewis
U.S.A.
CL, SB: Kathleen Lewis Beauty
D: James Dustin
P: David Herrenbruck

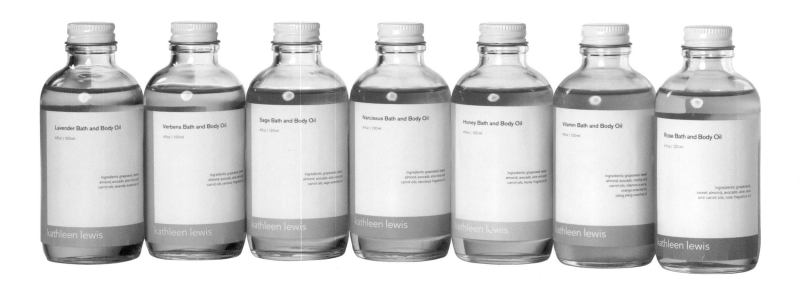

AROMA THERAPEUTICS
マロマセラピューティクス
U.K.
Japan agency, SB:
ビー・エル・オーバーシーズ (株)
B.L.Overseas co., ltd

daily delight
デイリーディライト
Japan
CL, SB: (株) グローバル プロダクト プランニング
Global Product Planning Co., Ltd.

Santa Maria Novella
サンタ・マリア・ノヴェッラ
Italy
CL, SB: サンタ・マリア・ノヴェッラ　Santa Maria Novella

Aēsop
イソップ
Australia
CL, SB: イソップ・ジャパン（株）Aēsop Japan KK

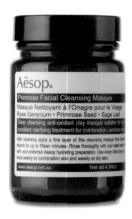

INSTITUT KARITE
カリテ
France
CL: カリテ社　INSTITUT KARITE

LE CHAT
レチャット
CL, SB: (有) ルーナーズ　LUNERS co., ltd

KORRES NATURAL PRODUCTS
コレスナチュラルプロダクト
Greece
CL, SB: (株) フィッツコーポレーション
FITS CORPORATION K.K.

THE BODY COLLECTION
ボディコレクション
Australia
CL: サックス インターナショナル　SAX International
SB:（有）三和トレーディング　SANWA TRADING INC.

daily delight
デイリーディライト
Japan
CL, SB: (株) グローバル プロダクト プランニング
Global Product Planning Co., Ltd.

MARIAS
マリアス
Austria
CL: ピーパー ナトゥア コスメティック マヌファクトゥア
Pieper Natur Cosmetic Manufaktur
D: Michael Nouri
SB: （株）インソーレ Insole & Co., Ltd.

ANNA SUI COSMETICS
アナ スイ コスメティックス
Japan
CL, SB: ㈱アルビオン　ALBION Co.,Ltd.
CD: アナ スイ　ANNA SUI
D: 中野 恵　Megumi Nakano / 石松 直子　Naoko Ishimatsu

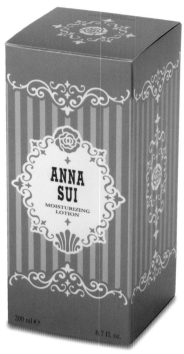

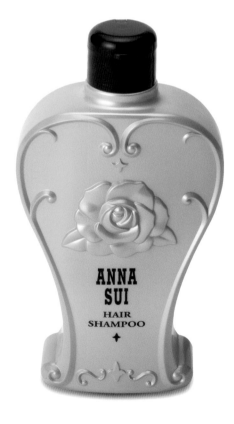

Loveliege
ラヴリージェ
Japan
CL, SB: (株) マーガレット・ジョセフィン・ジャパン
Margaret Josefin Co., Ltd.
D: 西邨 忠人　Tadahito Nishimura
DF: イズムデザインオフィス　ism design office

NERAIDA
ネライダ
Japan
CL, SB: (有) ドクターリュウズラボラトリー
Dr. Liu's Laboratory, Ltd.

ettusais
エテュセ
Japan
CL, SB: (株) エテュセ Et tu sais Co.,Ltd
CD, AD: 平林 奈緒美 Naomi Hirabayashi
D: 斗ヶ沢 哲雄 Tetsuo Togasawa (Bottle Design)
米山 菜津子 Natsuko Yoneyama (Label Design)

Natural House
ナチュラルハウス
Japan
CL: (株) ナチュラルハウス Natural House Co., Ltd.
CD, AD, D: 今井 クミ Kumi Imai
D: 塩澤 偉史 Yoshifumi Shiozawa
村上 奈緒子 Naoko Murakami
ART: 西田 真魚 Mao Nishida
DF, SB: アピスラボラトリー APIS LABORATORY INC.

AeSTA
エスタ
Japan
CL, SB: ファルフ（株）FALF INC.
D: 高橋 朗 Akira Takahashi

LAVALE
ラヴァーレ
Japan
CL, SB: (株) ユーア化学研究所　UA-chemical laboratory & co.
DF: (有) 青木デザイン事務所　aoki design office inc.

anuenue
アヌエヌエ
Japan
CL, SB: B&C ラボラトリーズ
B&C Laboratories Inc.

aroma new born
アロマ ニューボーン
New Zealand
CL: アロマ セラピー カンパニー　The Aromatherapy Company
SB: （有）三和トレーディング　SANWA TRADING INC.

RMK
アールエムケー
Japan
CL, SB: （株）エキップ　E'QUIPE, LTD.

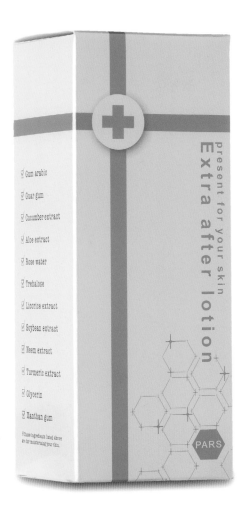

PARS EXTRA AFTER LOTION
パースエクストラアフターローション
Japan
CL, SB: ㈱パース　PARS CORPORATION
D: 中島 牧子　Makiko Nakajima

terre d'Oc
テールドック
France
CL, SB: ㈱ グローバル プロダクト プランニング
Global Product Planning Co., Ltd.

Panier des Sens
パニエ デ サンズ
France
CL: パニエ デ サンズ　Panier des Sens
SB: （有）三和トレーディング　SANWA TRADING INC.

Rituelle Lip Balm
リチュエル リップ バーム
Australia
CL: アーバンリチュエル　URBAN Rituelle
SB: (有) 三和トレーディング　SANWA TRADING INC.

Flower Fairies
フラワーフェアリーズ
CL, SB: (株) 日本グランド・シャンパーニュ
NIHON GRANDE CHAMPAGNE CO., LTD.

STEAM CREAM
スチームクリーム
Japan
CL, SB: エスシーコスメティクス（株） SC. Cosmetics Co., Ltd
D, AD: 戸塚 崇爲 Takayuki Totsuka
DF: トツカタカユキデザイン事務所 takayuki totsuka design office

SEXY GIRL
セクシーガール
Japan
CL, SB: （株）フィッツコーポレーション FITS CORPORATION K.K.
I: スギサキ メグミ Megumi Sugisaki

Makeup

LE WATOSA
ル ワトゥサ
Japan
CL, SB: ワトゥサ・インターナショナル
WATOSA International inc.
Brand director: 渡辺 サブロオ Sablo Watanabe

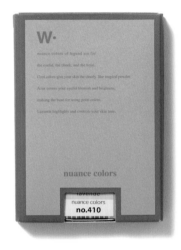

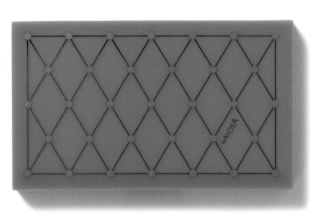

riches
リッチーズ
Japan
CL: (株) STARLET STARLET Inc.
AD: 村上 慶充 Yoshimitsu Murakami
DF: (株) クロスリング CROSS RING Inc.
SB: (株) ウィング WING co., LTD.

Mango   Royal Milk Tea   La France

Rich Hand Cream

www.e-riches.jp

Made in Tokyo

riches

Rich Gloss

Made in Tokyo

riches
Rich Body Butter
Royal Rose
Made in Tokyo

riches
Royal Rose

riches
Rich Body Butter
Tropical Fruits
Made in Tokyo

riches
Tropical Fruits

riches
Rich Body Butter
Honey Milk
Made in Tokyo

riches
Honey Milk

riches
Royal Milk Tea
Rich Hand Cream
Made in Tokyo
60g

riches
Rich Gloss
made in Tokyo
7g

Lavshuca
ラブーシュカ
Japan
CL, SB: ㈱カネボウ化粧品
Kanebo COSMETICS INC.

Marie Claire
マリ・クレール
Japan
CL, SB: コーセーコスメポート (株)
KOSÉ COSMEPORT

Diaphragma
ディアフラグマ
Japan
CL, SB: B&C ラボラトリーズ B&C Laboratories Inc.

Rosebud Salve, Minted Rose Lip Balm
ローズバット バーム　ミンティット ローズ リップ バーム
U.S.A.
CL, Design & Planning: ローズバット パフューム カンパニー　Rosebud Perfume Company, Inc
SB: (有) サンマリーノコレクション　San Marino Collection Co., Ltd.

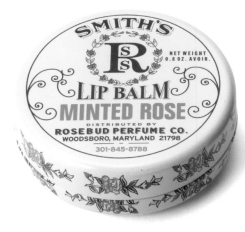

MAJOLICA MAJORCA
マジョリカ マジョルカ
Japan
CL, SB: (株) 資生堂 Shiseido Co., Ltd.
AD: 信藤 洋二 Yoji Nobuto
D: 近藤 香織 Kaori Kondo

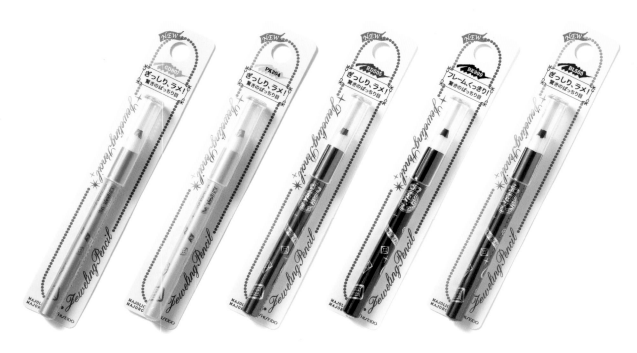

Para Do
パラドゥ
Japan
CL: パラドゥ（株） Para Do Corporation
CD: 齋藤 世織里 Seori Saito
AD: 若森 佐根治 Sakonji Wakamori
D: 栗栖 美幸 Miyuki Kurisu / 楊 裕幸 Hiroyuki Yo
DF: （株）ノイズ・バリュー社 NoIS Value Corporation
SB: ビアス（株） Pias Corpration

Tempted Sweets
テンプティッドスイーツ
CL, SB: （株）シュウエイトレーディング SHUEI TRADING CO.

BOURJOIS
ブルジョワ
France
CL, SB: ブルジョワ（株）Bourjois Paris

Mary Rose Collection

All natural lip care tint

Natural Looking Lip Tint

Mary Rose Collection
マリーローズ コレクション
U.S.A.
CL, Planning, SB:（有）サンマリーノコレクション
San Marino Collection Co., Ltd.
D: 作山 博美　Hiromi Sakuyama

Mary Rose Collection

Lip Cha Cha
Lip Bliss

Yummy!!! Matcha flavor

Mary Rose Collection

Aura Mineral
Loose Powder

Matcha tea Scented
Hand Cha Cha
Hand Balm

Nourishment in
Green tea Extract
Rich with
Shea Butter

Ganache For Lips
ガナッシュ・フォー・リップス
U.S.A.
CL, SB: ㈱ シュウエイトレーディング
SHUEI TRADING CO.

HOLLYWOOD LIPS
ハリウッドリップス
U.S.A.
CL, SB: ㈱ ジョージオリバー George & Oliver Co., ltd.

SAKURA
さくら
Japan
CL, SB: (株) スリースタイル　three style co., ltd.
D: 加納 彩人　Akihito Kanoh
DF: NIN デザイン　NIN design

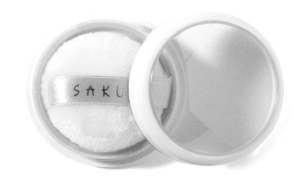

Cura
キューラ
Japan
CL, SB: アドム（株）Adom Co., ltd
D: 和田 浩次郎 Kojro Wada
DF: （有）ケイズデザイン K's design Inc.

B NEVER TOO BUSY TO BE
BEAUTIFUL
ビーネバートゥービジートゥービービューティフル
Japan, India (Package)
CL, SB: ビーネバートゥービジートゥービービューティフル（株）
B never too busy to be beautiful Co., Ltd

Fragrance

PACIFICA
パシフィカ
U.S.A.
CL, SB: ㈱日本香堂 NIPPON KODO CO.,LTD.

terre d'Oc
テールドック
France
CL, SB: (株) グローバル プロダクト プランニング
Global Product Planning Co., Ltd.

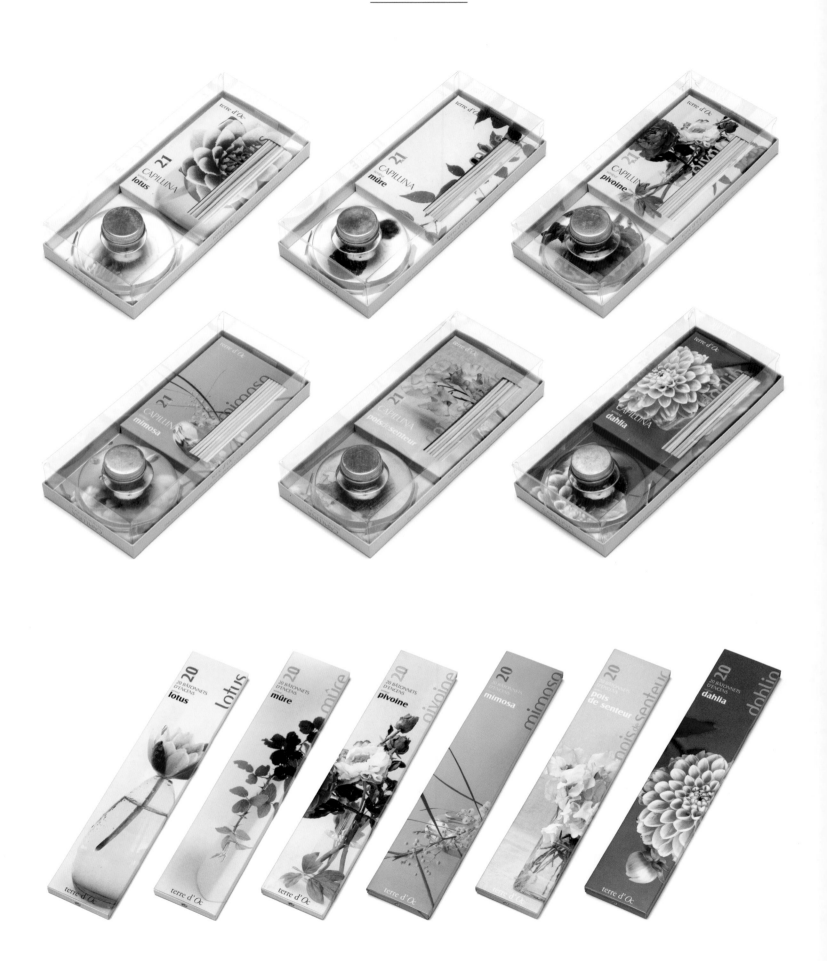

Garden Party
ガーデンパーティ
Australia
CL: アーバンリチュエル URBAN Rituelle
SB: (有) 三和トレーディング SANWA TRADING INC.

RANCÉ
ランセ
France
CL, SB: (株) フォルテ Forte. Co., Ltd.

fragrant JOURNEY

フレグラントジャーニー
Australia
CL: アーバンリチュエル URBAN Rituelle
SB: (有)三和トレーディング SANWA TRADING INC.

Love passport
ラブパスポート
Japan
CL, SB:（株）フィッツコーポレーション
FITS CORPORATION K.K.
D: 野田 凪 Nagi Noda / 吉田 ユニ Yuni Yoshida

LUCKY CHARM
ラッキーチャーム
Japan
CL, SB: ㈱ グローバル プロダクト プランニング
Global Product Planning Co., Ltd.

Lulu Rose
ルルローズ
Japan
CL, SB: （株）グローバル プロダクト プランニング
Global Product Planning Co., Ltd.

Souris Verte
スーリ・ヴェール
France
CL, SB: (株) フォルテ Forte. Co., Ltd.

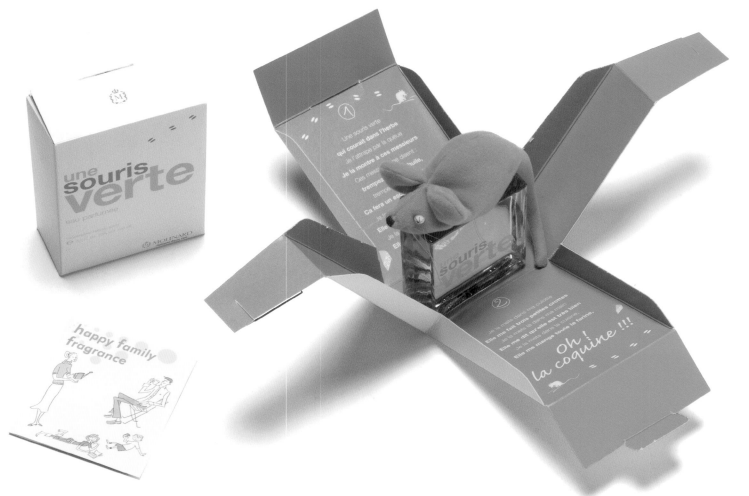

jacadi PARIS
ジャカディ パリ
France
CL, SB: （株）フォルテ Forte. Co., Ltd.

Flarde
フラーデ
Japan
CL, SB: ㈱美健　BIKEN Co.
D: 柴田 和人　Kazuhito Shibata

Happyholic

ハッピーホリック

France

CL, SB: ㈱ エクスパンド　EXpand Co., Ltd.

D: オオノ リョウスケ　Ryosuke Ohno

Room Fragrance

ルームフレグランス

Japan

CL, SB: ㈱ ローレル　LAUREL CO., LTD.

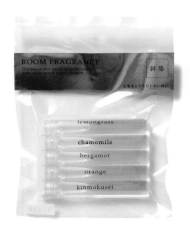

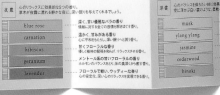

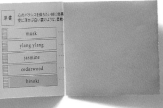

ABAHNA
アバーナ
U.K.
CL, SB: ㈱フィッツコーポレーション
FITS CORPORATION K.K.
D: クレア・クロフ　Claire Croft

MATHIAS
マティアス
France
CL,SB: （株）フィッツコーポレーション
FITS CORPORATION K.K.

VOTIVO
ボーティボ
U.S.A.
CL,SB: ㈱ グローバル プロダクト プランニング
Global Product Planning Co., Ltd.

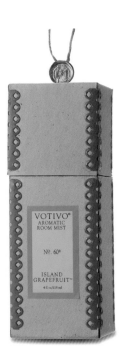

ESTEBAN
エステバン
France
CL, SB: (株) 日本香堂　NIPPON KODO CO.,LTD.

ESTEBAN
エステバン
France
CL, SB: ㈱日本香堂　NIPPON KODO CO.,LTD.

Tonnelle et lilas

Bower and lilac

recharge pour bouquet parfumé
scented bouquet refill

ESTEBAN
PARIS

Rose du matin

Morning rose

recharge pour bouquet parfumé
scented bouquet refill

ESTEBAN
PARIS

Pêche de vigne

Vineyard peach

recharge pour bouquet parfumé
scented bouquet refill

ESTEBAN
PARIS

Divin Jasmin

Heavenly jasmine

recharge pour bouquet parfumé
scented bouquet refill

ESTEBAN
PARIS

Figuier Tardif

Late summer fig

recharge pour bouquet parfumé
scented bouquet refill

ESTEBAN
PARIS

Fleurs d'Oranger

Orange blossoms

recharge pour bouquet parfumé
refill scented bouquet

ESTEBAN
PARIS

ESTEBAN
エステバン
France
CL, SB: ㈱日本香堂　NIPPON KODO CO.,LTD.

nonohana
ののはな
Japan
CL, SB: （株）グローバル プロダクト プランニング
Global Product Planning Co., Ltd.

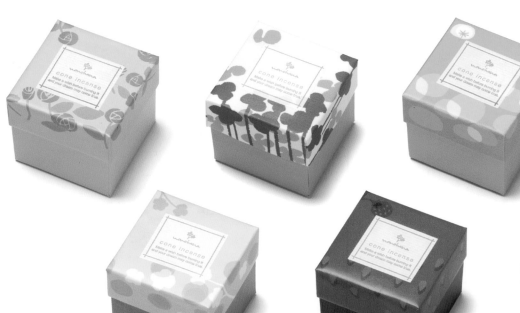

fav
ファヴ
Japan
CL, SB: （株）グローバル プロダクト プランニング
Global Product Planning Co., Ltd.

rose
Soft & heartwarming scent

cone incense
you will surely find your favorite fragrance

ange
Cute and happy scent

cone incense
you will surely find your favorite fragrance

peach
Juicy fresh scent

cone incense
you will surely find your favorite fragrance

papaya
Fresh and sweet scent

cone incense
you will surely find your favorite fragrance

white musk
Tender scent of musk

cone incense
you will surely find your favorite fragrance

lavender
Refreshing & Calming scent

cone incense
you will surely find your favorite fragrance

synchronicity
Scent of musk with floral touch

cone incense
you will surely find your favorite fragrance

french vanilla
Sweet and mild scent

cone incense
you will surely find your favorite fragrance

rainy musk
Crystal-clear musk scent

cone incense
you will surely find your favorite fragrance

grass
Scent of invigorating wind

cone incense
you will surely find your favorite fragrance

coconut
Relaxing scent of Tropical island

cone incense
you will surely find your favorite fragrance

sea blue
Fresh scent of seaside breeze

cone incense
you will surely find your favorite fragrance

DAIRY AROMA
デイリーアロマ
Japan
CL, SB: ㈱美健 BIKEN Co.
D: 柴田 和人 Kazuhito Shibata

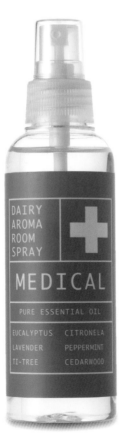

SABON
サボン
State of Israel
CL, SB: ㈱ SABON Japan　SABON Japan

Violette Cherie
ヴィオレット・シェリー
France
CL, SB: ㈱フォルテ Forte. Co., Ltd.

Creature d' Anges
クレアチュール・アンジ
France
CL, SB: ㈱フォルテ Forte. Co., Ltd.

Le Petit Prince
星の王子さま〜ヒツジの絵を描いて〜
France
CL, SB: (株) フォルテ　Forte. Co., Ltd.

FIANCÉE
フィアンセ
Japan
CL, SB: （株）井田ラボラトリーズ
IDA Laboratories Co., Ltd.

sweets sweets
スウィーツ スウィーツ
Japan
CL, SB: （株）セザンヌ化粧品
CEZANNE COSMETICS Co., Ltd.

yawaragi
和
Japan
CL, SB: （株）グローバル プロダクト プランニング
Global Product Planning Co., Ltd.

NON-SMOKE INCENSE
無煙香
Japan
CL, SB: ㈱美健　BIKEN Co.
D: 小笠原 志織　Shiori Ogasawara

Resort Aroma
リゾートアロマ
Japan
CL, SB: ㈱美健　BIKEN Co.
D: 奥津 美香　Mika Okutsu

nk pure
エヌケーピュア
Japan
CL, SB: （株）日本香堂　NIPPON KODO CO.,LTD.

Hair-care

LUCIDO-L
ルシードエル
Japan
CL, SB: (株)マンダム mandom corp.

P.SUIT
ピースーツ
Japan
CL, SB: （株）ナンバースリー　NUMBER THREE, INC.
D: 峠田 充謙　Mitsunori Taoda

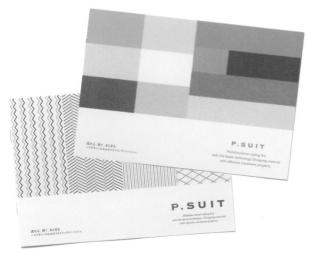

DESIGN TEX
クリエイター デザインテックス
Japan
CL, SB: 資生堂プロフェッショナル（株） SHISEIDO PROFESSIONAL INC.
CD: 足立 和彦　エフ クリエイション（株） Kazuhiko Adachi　F CREATION CO., LTD.
D: 伊藤 透 Toru Ito
DF: TORU ITO DESIGN

DEUXER
デューサー
Japan
CL, SB: （株）ナンバースリー　NUMBER THREE, INC.
D: 峠田 充謙　Mitsunori Taoda

Glatty Matty
グラッティ マッティ
Japan
CL, SB: (株) ナンバースリー
NUMBER THREE, INC.
D: 峠田 充謙 Mitsunori Taoda

Liese
リーゼ
Japan
CL, SB: 花王（株）
Kao Corporation

Schwarzkopf Professional
シュワルツコフプロフェッショナル
Japan
CL, SB: ヘンケルジャパン（株）
シュワルツコフプロフェッショナル
Henkel Japan Ltd.
Schwarzkopf Professional division
D, I: 後藤 美和　Miwa Goto

mint
ミント
Japan
CL, SB: （株）アリミノ　ARIMINO Co.,ltd.
DF: （株）アナザー・レポート　Another Report Co.,ltd.

TRISYS
トリシス
Japan
CL, SB: ㈱ナンバースリー NUMBER THREE, INC.
D: 峠田 充謙 Mitsunori Taoda

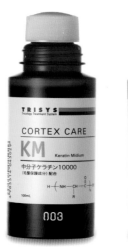

MARGARET JOSEFIN
マーガレット・ジョセフィン
Japan
CL, SB: (株) マーガレット・ジョセフィン・ジャパン
Margaret Josefin Co., Ltd.
D: 西邨 忠人　Tadahito Nishimura
DF: イズムデザインオフィス　ism design office
PRODUCER: 牧野 琢弥　Takuya Makino

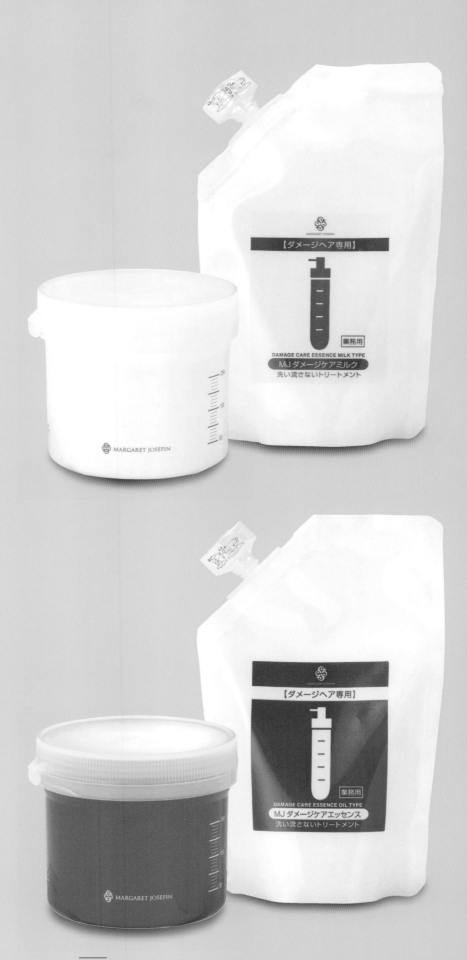

L'OCCITANE
ロクシタン
France
CL, SB: ロクシタン ジャポン（株）
L'OCCITANE JAPON K.K.

BROAD hair
ブロードヘア
Japan
CL, SB: ㈱ビーロード Broad Co., Ltd.
D: 徳田 淳 Jun Tokuda

Vigour Energy Shampoo
Russia
CL: Neoform Health&Beauty, Moscow, Russia
D, SB: Oleg Lukyanov

HAIR SEASONS
ヘアシーズンズ
Japan
CL, SB: 日華化学（株）
デミ コスメティクス
NICCA CHEMICAL CO.,LTD.
DEMI COSMETICS
D: 向後 敦 Atsushi Cogo
DF: （株）クーグー CooGoo

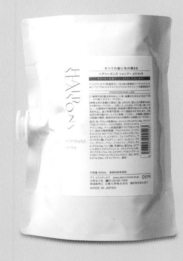

RENASCENT
リナセント
Japan
CL, SB: 資生堂プロフェッショナル（株）SHISEIDO PROFESSIONAL INC.
CD: 池田 修一　エフ クリエイション（株）Shuichi Ikeda　F CREATION CO., LTD.
D: 工藤 青石　Aoshi Kudo
DF: コミュニケーションデザイン研究所　Communication Design Laboratory

digna
デザインフレックス ディグナ
Japan
CL, SB: 資生堂プロフェッショナル（株）SHISEIDO PROFESSIONAL INC.
D: 高橋 伸幸　Nobuyuki Takahashi
DF: スリーミン・グラフィック・アソシエイツ　3Min. Graphic Associates

Bath Products

Côté Bastide
コテ バスティド
France
CL: コテ バスティド Côté Bastide
D: ニコル・ウーク Nicole Houques
SB: （株）林タオル フランジュール事業部
HAYASHI TOWEL CO., LTD. FRANCJOUR DIV.

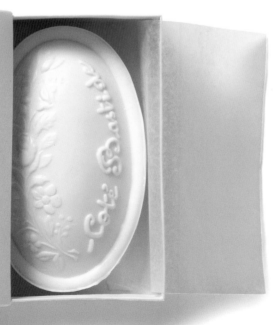

Côté Bastide
コテ バスティド
France
CL: コテ バスティド Côté Bastide
D: ニコル・ウーク Nicole Houques
SB: ㈱林タオル フランジュール事業部
HAYASHI TOWEL CO., LTD. FRANCJOUR DIV.

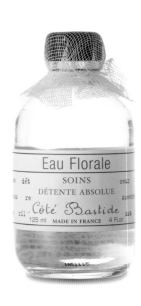

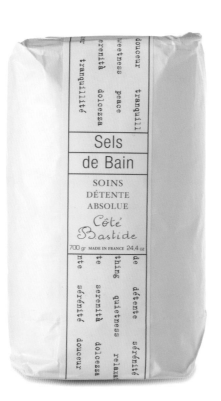

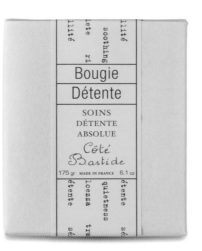

LEAF & BOTANICS
リーフ & ボタニクス
Japan
CL, SB: 松山油脂 (株) Matsuyama Co., Ltd.
CD: 松山 剛己 Tsuyoshi Matsuyama
D: 熊野 由 Yuki Kumano

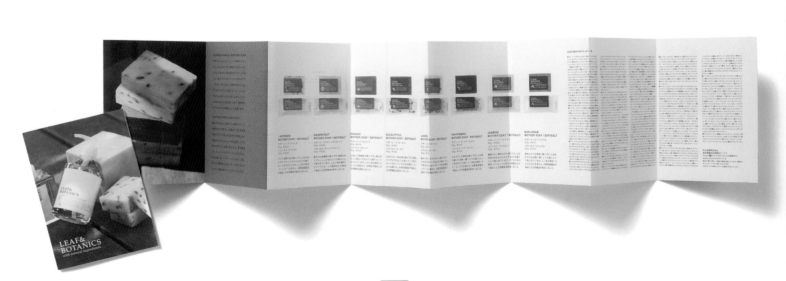

LEAF & BOTANICS

リーフ & ボタニクス
Japan
CL, SB: 松山油脂（株）Matsuyama Co., Ltd.
CD: 松山 剛己 Tsuyoshi Matsuyama
D: 熊野 由 Yuki Kumano

LE SÉ RAIL
ル セライユ
France
CL, SB: （株）グローバル プロダクト プランニング
Global Product Planning Co., Ltd.

Florame
フローラム
France
CL, SB: （株）サンテ・クレール　Santé Claire Inc.

Florame
フローラム
France
CL, SB: ㈱サンテ・クレール Santé Claire Inc.

IKOVE
イコヴェ
Brasil
CL, SB: （株）フロレスタス・ジャパン　FLORESTAS JAPAN INC.
D: Collin Liu
DF: Particle-visual design

YUUYOO
ユーヨー
Japan
CL,SB: ㈱ インナチュラル IN NATURAL Co., Ltd.

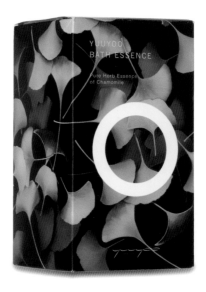

Sufu
スフ
Japan
CL, SB: (株) ペリカン石鹸 Pelican Soap Co. Ltd.
D: 福島 よし恵 Yoshie Fukushima

THERMAE DI SALSOMAGGIORE
テルメ ディ サルソマッジョーレ
Italy
CL, SB: （株）アリエルトレーディング　Ariel Trading Co., ltd.

LA COMPAGNIE DE PROVENCE
ラ カンパニードプロバンス ラグゼ
France
CL, SB: （株）グローバル プロダクト プランニング
Global Product Planning Co., Ltd.

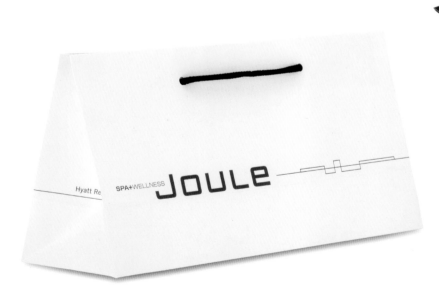

JOULE
ジュール
Japan
CL, SB: ハイアット リージェンシー 東京
HYATT REGENCY TOKYO

elizabethW
エリザベスダヴリュー
U.S.A.
CL,SB:（株）グローバル プロダクト プランニング
Global Product Planning Co., Ltd.

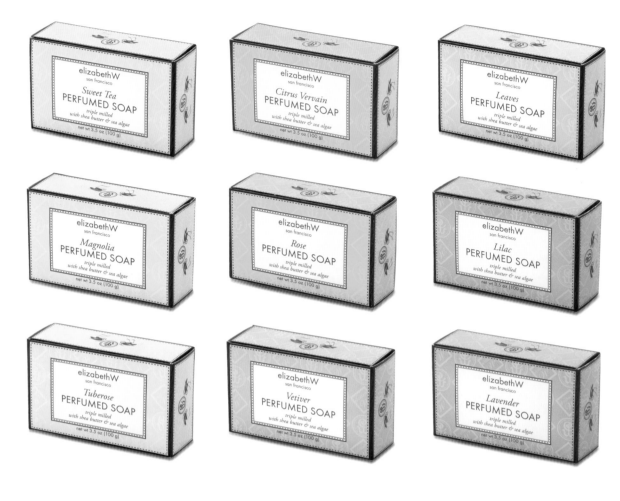

SUNHERB
サンハーブ
CL,SB: (株) グローバル プロダクト プランニング
Global Product Planning Co., Ltd.

Organic Botanicals
オーガニック ボタニカルズ
Japan
CL, SB: (株) クリークグローバル Creek Global Co., Ltd.
D: 米谷 育子 Ikuko Yonetani

NESTI DANTE
ネスティ・ダンテ
Italy
CL, SB: (株) 日本グランド・シャンパーニュ
NIHON GRANDE CHAMPAGNE CO., LTD.

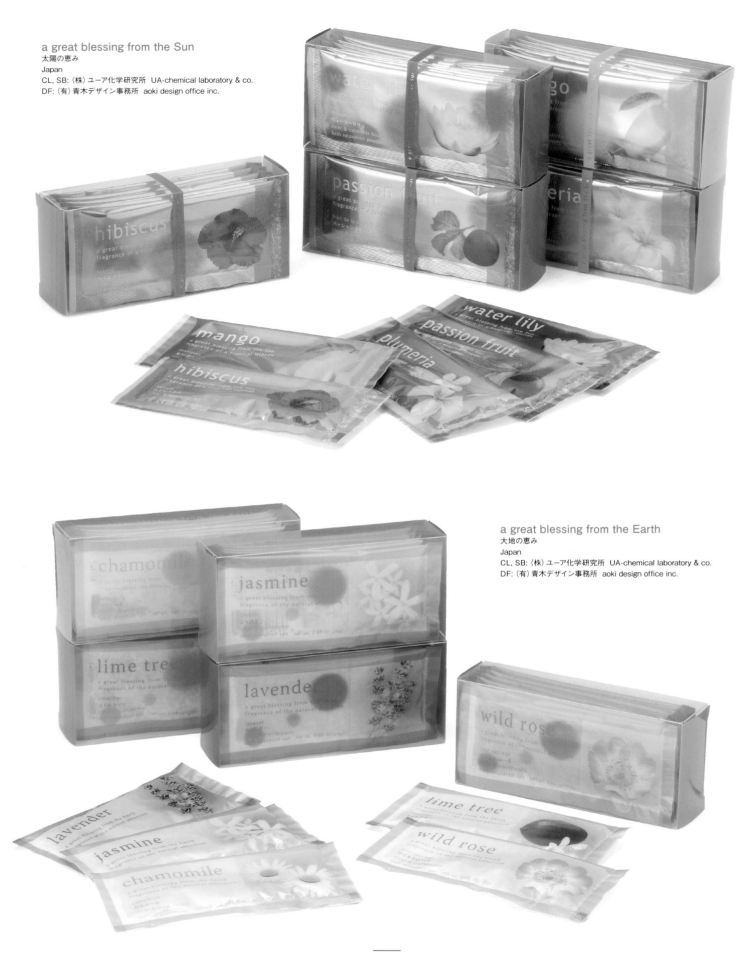

a great blessing from the Sun
太陽の恵み
Japan
CL, SB: （株）ユーア化学研究所　UA-chemical laboratory & co.
DF: （有）青木デザイン事務所　aoki design office inc.

a great blessing from the Earth
大地の恵み
Japan
CL, SB: （株）ユーア化学研究所　UA-chemical laboratory & co.
DF: （有）青木デザイン事務所　aoki design office inc.

Natural Aroma
ナチュラル アロマ
Japan
CL, SB: ㈱ユーア化学研究所 UA-chemical laboratory & co.
DF: ㈲青木デザイン事務所 aoki design office inc.

bath selection Fruity bath
バスセレクション
Japan
CL, SB: ㈱ユーア化学研究所 UA-chemical laboratory & co.
DF: ㈲青木デザイン事務所 aoki design office inc.

Beans Soap
ビーンズソープ
Japan
CL, SB: （株）ローレル　LAUREL CO., LTD.

ZOOCOS. Tokyo
ズーコス トーキョー
Japan
CL, SB: （株）アイデープロジェクト　ID PROJECT. CO. LTD
D: Mioh

FRAGRANT GARDEN
フレグラント ガーデン
Japan
CL, SB: (株) ユーア化学研究所 UA-chemical laboratory & co.
DF: (有) 青木デザイン事務所 aoki design office inc.

bath selection classic
バスセレクション クラシック 風雅
Japan
CL, SB: (株) ユーア化学研究所 UA-chemical laboratory & co.
DF: (株) アイディーエイ 岡山オフィス IDA inc.

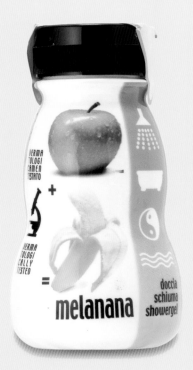

athena's
アテナ
Italy
CL, SB: ㈱日本グランド・シャンパーニュ
NIHON GRANDE CHAMPAGNE CO., LTD.

GIANNA ROSE ATELIER
ジアンナ ローズ アトリエ
U.S.A.
CL, SB: (株) グローバル プロダクト プランニング
Global Product Planning Co., Ltd.

LAVEA
ラベア
Czech
CL,SB: (株) AMADEUS　AMADEUS Co., Ltd.

Fin rose Bath soak

White birch Bath soak

Hay flower Bath soak

Aurora Orange Bath soak

FINLAND Series
フィンランドシリーズ
Japan
CL, SB: ㈱チャーリー CHARLEY CO., LTD

Canadian Spa
カナディアンスパ
Japan
CL, SB: ㈱美健 BIKEN Co.
D: 柴田 和人 Kazuhito Shibata

crystallixation
クリスタリゼーション
Japan
CL, SB: ㈱ユーア化学研究所 UA-chemical laboratory & co.
DF: ㈲青木デザイン事務所 aoki design office inc.

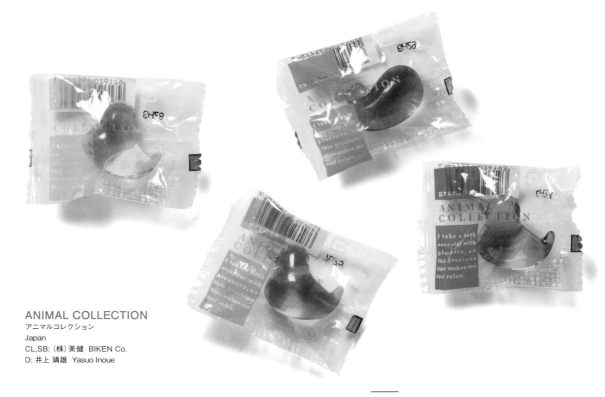

ANIMAL COLLECTION
アニマルコレクション
Japan
CL,SB: ㈱美健 BIKEN Co.
D: 井上 靖雄 Yasuo Inoue

目立つな、毛色

目立ちたがり屋のモジャに告ぐバスソルト

熟れよ、女の武器(ウエポン)

引っ込み思案な色気に告ぐバスソルト

蘇れ、赤子肌(カムバック)

曲がり角を過ぎたお肌に告ぐバスソルト

捕まえよ、王子

お姫様志願の乙女心に告ぐバスソルト

来たれ、熱汗

ただいま冬眠中の汗に告ぐバスソルト

くたばるな、わが身

嘆くわが身に告ぐバスソルト

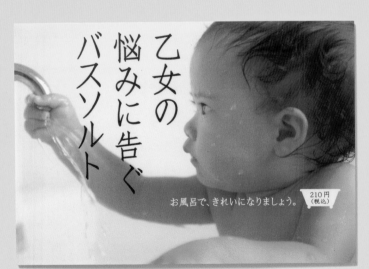

乙女の悩みに告ぐバスソルト

お風呂で、きれいになりましょう。

210円（税込）

P.O.P.

OTOME NO NAYAMI BATH
乙女の悩みに告ぐバスソルト
Japan
CL, SB: (株)ローレル

Ehon bath bag
絵本バスバック
Japan
CL, SB: ㈱チャーリー CHARLEY CO., LTD

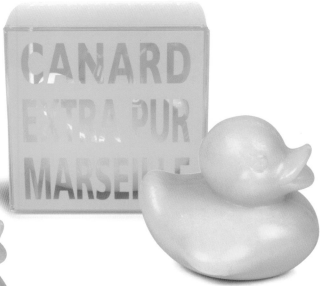

LA COMPAGNIE DE PROVENCE
ラ カンパニードプロバンス
France
CL, SB: ㈱ グローバル プロダクト プランニング Global Product Planning Co., Ltd.

sakura
桜
Japan
CL,SB: (株) グローバル プロダクト プランニング
Global Product Planning Co., Ltd.

KURAKUYU
くらくゆ
Japan
CL, SB: (有) 句楽 KURAKU Co.,Ltd.

aqua scape
アクアスケープ
Japan
CL, SB: ㈱ユーア化学研究所 UA-chemical laboratory & co.
DF: ㈲青木デザイン事務所 aoki design office inc.

ESTHE JELLY
エステゼリー
Japan
CL, SB: ㈱タフリーインターナショナル
TOU-FREE INTERNATIONAL CO.,LTD.
D: 加賀 美保 Miho Kaga
P: 脇谷 隆介 Ryusuke Wakitani
DF: 加賀デザイン事務所 KAGA DESIGN ROOM

BABAGHURI
ババグーリ
Japan
CL, SB: ヨーガン レール　JURGEN LEHL CO. LTD.
D, P: ヨーガン レール（石鹸）　JURGEN LEHL
P: 小泉 佳春（シャンプー，リンス）Yoshiharu Koizumi

Kaivola farm
カイボラファーム
Finland
CL, SB: トロイヤー・フント　TREUER HUND ltd.

Supplement, Others

METHOD
メソッド
U.S.A.
CL, SB: K-フラッグ（株）
K-Flag Co. ltd

Fabric Water
ファブリックウォーター
Japan
CL, SB: ㈱美健　BIKEN Co.
D: 柴田 和人　Kazuhito Shibata

Florame
フローラム
France
CL, SB: ㈱サンテ・クレール
Santé Claire Inc.

aq-01, aq-02, aq-03
エーキューゼロイチ , エーキューゼロニ , エーキューゼロサン
Japan
CL: アークレイ（株）ARKRAY, Inc.
D: 北川 一成 Issay Kitagawa
DF, SB: グラフ（株）GRAPH CO.,LTD.

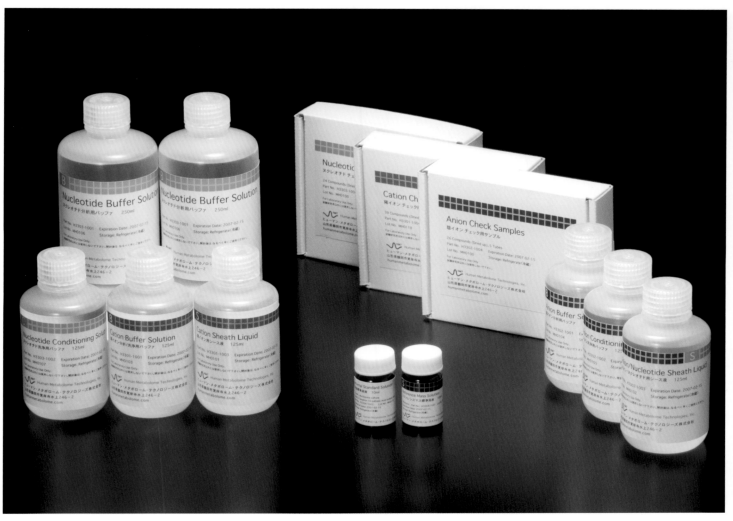

HUMAN METABOLOME TECHNOLOGIES
ヒューマン・メタボローム・テクノロジーズ
Japan
CL: ヒューマン・メタボローム・テクノロジーズ（株）
HUMAN METABOLOME TECHNOLOGIES, INC.
D, SB: ウノサワ ケイスケ　Keisuke Unosawa
DF: OPERA, Inc.

ORBIS
オルビス
CL, SB: オルビス（株）　ORBIS Inc.

BREATH PALETTE WATER excellent
ブレスパレットウォーター
CL, SB: (株) マーガレット・ジョセフィン・ジャパン
Margaret Josefin Co., Ltd.
DF: (有) ドラゴンフライ　DRAGONFLY

Dr.Ci:Labo
ドクターシーラボ
Japan
CL, SB: (株) ドクターシーラボ
Dr.Ci:Labo Co., Ltd.

Honey Cube
ハニーキューブ
Japan
CL, SB: (株) チャーリー CHARLEY CO., LTD

HERBAN ESSENTIALS
ハーバーエッセンシャルズ
U.S.A.
CL, SB: ㈱アリエルトレーディング
Ariel Trading Co., ltd

RMK
アールエムケー
Japan
CL, SB: ㈱エキップ E'QUIPE, LTD.

Dr. BAELTZ
ドクターベルツ
Japan
CL, SB: ドクターベルツ　Dr. BAELTZ Co. ltd.

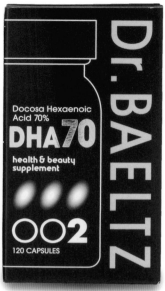
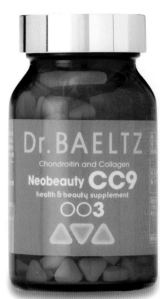
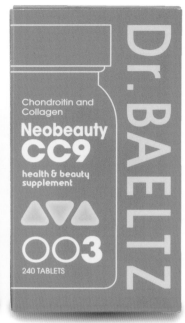

SUPPLY PALETTE
サプリパレット
Japan
CL, SB: （株）マーガレット・ジョセフィン・ジャパン
Margaret Josefin Co., Ltd.
D: 西邨 忠人　Tadahito Nishimura
DF: イズムデザインオフィス　ism design office

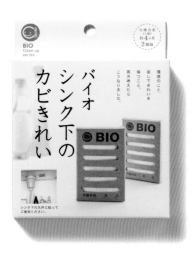

COGIT
コジット
Japan
CL, SB: （株）コジット　COGIT Co., Ltd.

INDEX

CLIENTS INDEX

クライアントリスト

SUBMITTORS INDEX

出品者リスト

CLIENTS INDEX　クライアントリスト

SUBMITTORS INDEX 出品者リスト

コスメ&ヘルスケア パッケージデザイン
Beauty and Healthcare Package Design

Jacket Design, Title Page
Art Director: カイシ トモヤ (room-composite)　Tomoya Kaishi (room-composite)
Designer: 大垣 江美　Emi Ogaki

Art Director
柴 亜季子　Akiko Shiba

Designer
ウエマツ ノボル　Noboru Uematsu
林 国和　Kunikazu Hayashi

Photographer
藤本 邦治　Kuniharu Fujimoto

Translator
パメラ ミキ　Pamela Miki

Coordinator
安井 克至　Katsuyuki Yasui
吉田 香織　Kaori Yoshida

Editor
斉藤 香　Kaori Saito

Publisher
三芳 伸吾　Shingo Miyoshi

2008 年 12 月 10 日　初版第 1 刷発行

PIE BOOKS
2-32-4, Minami-Otsuka, Toshima-ku, Tokyo 170-0005 JAPAN
Tel: +81-3-5395-4811　Fax : +81-3-5395-4812
e-mail: editor@piebooks.com　sales@piebooks.com
http://www.piebooks.com

発行所　ピエ・ブックス
170-0005 東京都豊島区南大塚 2-32-4

営業　Tel: 03-5395-4811　Fax : 03-5395-4812
　　　sales@piebooks.com

編集　Tel: 03-5395-4820　Fax : 03-5395-4821
　　　editor@piebooks.com

　　　http://www.piebooks.com

印刷・製本　株式会社サンニチ印刷

IN-STORE DISPLAY GRAPHICS

店頭コミュニケーショングラフィックス

Page: 216 (Full Color) ￥14,000+Tax

店頭でのプロモーション展開においては、空間デザインだけでなくグラフィックデザインが果たす役割も重要です。本書では、空間のイメージとグラフィックツールのコンセプトが一貫している作品をはじめ、限られたスペースで有効活用できるディスプレーキットや、P.O.P.の役割も果たすショップツールなどを広く紹介します。

995

A useful display tool for a limited space, display examples which show the harmonization among packaging, shop interior and in-store promotional graphics, a creative point-of-sale tool which stands out among others. This book is a perfect resource for designers and marketing professionals.

CHARACTER DESIGN TODAY

キャラクターデザイン・トゥデイ

Page: 232 (Full Color) ￥14,000+Tax

キャラクターは企業と消費者とを結ぶ有効なコミュニケーションツールといえます。競合商品との差別化をはかるため、企業のサービスを消費者にわかりやすく伝えるためなど、その役割は様々です。本書では、キャラクターのデザインコンセプト、プロフィールとともに広告やツールの展開例を収録。巻頭では、キャラクターが決定するまでの過程やボツ案を特集し、長く愛されるキャラクターをデザインするポイントを探ります。

984

200 successful characters with each profile, concept as well as the graphic examples. A featured article about the process of creating a character from scratch is also included with useful examples.

PACKAGE FORM AND DESIGN

ペーパーパッケージデザイン大全集　作例＆展開図(CD-ROM付)

Page: 240 (Full Color) ￥7,800+Tax

大好評の折り方シリーズ第3弾。製品を守りブランドアイデンティティーのアピールとなるパッケージ。本書ではバラエティーに富んだかたちのペーパーパッケージ約200点を国内外から集め、その作例と展開図を紹介していきます。展開図を掲載したCD-ROM付きでクリエイターやパッケージ制作に関わる人たちの参考資料として永久保存版の1冊です。

941

This is the third title focusing on paper packaging in "Encyclopedia of Paper Folding Design" series. The 150 high quality works are all created by the industry professionals; the perfect shapes and beautiful designs are practical and yet artistic. The template files in pdf file on CD-ROM.

DESIGN IDEAS FOR RENEWAL

再生グラフィックス

Page: 240 (Full Color) ￥14,000+Tax

本書では"再生"をキーワードにデザインの力で既存の商業地や施設、ブランドを甦らせた事例を特集します。リニューアル後のグラフィックツールを中心に、デザインコンセプトや再生後の効果についても紹介します。企業や地域の魅力を再活性させるためにデザインが果たした役割を実感できる1冊です。

977

A collection of case studies - with "regeneration" and "renewal" as their keywords - showing commercial districts, facilities and brands brought back to life through the power of design. Focusing on mainly the post-renovation graphic tools, we present the design concepts and their regenerative effects through which readers will see the role that design can play in reigniting the allure of companies and communities.

GIRLY GRAPHICS

ガーリー グラフィックス

Page: 200 (Full Color) ￥9,800+Tax

"ガーリー"とは女の子らしさの見直しや、ポップでありながらもキュートといった、女の子らしさを楽しむポジティブな姿勢を意味します。そんな"ガーリー"な空気感を、ポスター・DM・カタログ・パッケージなどのデザイン領域で、魅力的に表現した作品を紹介します。

1009

A word "girly" represents an expression of reconstructing positive images about being girls. Today, those powerful and contagious "girly" images with great impact successfully grab attentions not only from girls but also from a broad range of audience. This book features about those 300 enchanted and fascinated advertisements such as posters, catalogs, shop cards, business cards, books, CD jackets, greeting cards, letterheads, product packages and more.

NEO JAPANESQUE DESIGN

ネオ ジャパネスク デザイン

Page: 224 (Full Color) ￥14,000+Tax

2006年2月に発刊し好評を得た「ネオ ジャパネスク グラフィックス」。待望の第二弾「ネオ ジャパネスク デザイン」がいよいよ登場。ショップイメージ・ロゴ＆マークのカテゴリが新たに加わり、内容・クオリティともにバージョンアップした"和"デザインの最前線を紹介します。

996

This is the sister edition to "Neo Japanesque Graphics" published in 2006, and this new book includes even more modern yet Japanese taste designs which will give creative professionals inspirational ideas for their projects. Among various graphic works, this second title features shop design such as restaurants, bars and hotels, also features a variety of Japanese logos.

文字を読ませる広告デザイン 2

Page: 192 (Full Color) ￥9,800+Tax

パッと見た時に文字が目に入ってきて、しかも読みやすいデザインの広告物やパッケージの特集です。優れたデザインや文字組み、コピーによって見る側に文字・文章を読ませることを第一に考えられた広告を厳選します。ポスター、新聞広告、チラシ、車内吊り、雑誌広告、DM、カタログ、パンフレット、本の装丁、パッケージ、看板・サインなど多岐なジャンルにわたり紹介します。

934

Sales in Japan only.

FASHION BRAND GRAPHICS

ファッション グラフィックス

Page: 160 (Full Color) ￥7,800+Tax

本書は、ファッション、アパレルにおけるグラフィックデザインに力を入れた販促ツールを、厳選して紹介します。通常のショップツールはもちろん、シーズンごとと、キャンペーンごとのツールも掲載。激しく移り変わるファッション業界において、お客様を飽きさせない、華やかで魅力的な作品を凝縮した1冊です。

962

The fashion brands that appear in this collection are among the most highly regarded in Japan and herein we introduce some of their commonly used marketing tools including catalogues, shopping cards and shopping bags, together with their seasonal promotional tools and novelties. This publication serves for not only graphic designers, but also people in the fashion industry, marketing professionals.

GRAPHIC SIMPLICITY

シンプル グラフィックス

Page: 248 (Full Color)　¥14,000+Tax

上質でシンプルなデザイン — 見た目がすっきりとして美しいのはもちろんのこと、シンプルなのに個性的な作品、カラフルなのに上品な作品、フォントやロゴがさりげなく効いている作品など、その洗練されたデザインは見る人を魅了してやみません。本書は厳選された作品を国内外から集め、落ち着いた大人の雰囲気にまとめ上げた本物志向のグラフィックコレクションです。

Simple, high-quality design work: not just crisply elegant and eye catching, but uncluttered yet distinctive, colorful yet refined, making subtly effective use of fonts and logos; in short, sophisticated design that seduces all who sees it.

973

BEST FLYER 365DAYS NEWSPAPER INSERT EDITION

ベストチラシ 365 デイズ　折込チラシ編

Page: 256 (Full Color)　¥14,000+Tax

一番身近な広告媒体である新聞の折込チラシ。地域に密着したお得な情報を提供するものから、セレブ＆クールで夢のようなビジュアルのものまで多種多様です。本書では、1年間 (365日) の各セールスシーズンでまとめたものから、1枚だけで効果的に商品をPRしたチラシまで、優れたデザインの旬な折込チラシ800点を収録しています。広告の制作に携わる人びとに必携のデザインサンプル集です。

This book contains many examples of excellently designed, topical flyers, ranging from seasonal advertisements to flyers for a single product. It is an anthology of design samples for creative professionals in the advertising industry.

936

1&2 COLOR EDITORIAL DESIGN

1・2色でみせるエディトリアルデザイン

Page: 160 (Full Color)　¥7,800+Tax

少ない色数でエディトリアルデザインする際には、写真の表現や本文使用色に制限がある分、レイアウトや使用する紙に工夫や表現力が問われます。本書は1色、2色で魅力的にレイアウトされた作品を、インクや用紙データのスペックと併せて紹介します。

This book presents many of well-selected editorial design examples, featuring unique and outstanding works using one or two colors. All works in this single volume present designers enormous hints for effective and unique techniques with information on specs of inks and papers. Examples include PR pamphlets, magazines, catalogs, company brochures, and books.

956

BEYOND ADVERTISING: COMMUNICATION DESIGN

コミュニケーション デザイン

Page: 224 (Full Color)　¥15,000+Tax

限られた予算のなか、ターゲットへ確実に届く、費用対効果の高い広告をどのように実現するか？ 今デザイナーには、広告デザインだけでなく、コミュニケーション方法までもデザインすることが求められています。本書では「消費者との新しいコミュニケーションのカタチ」をテーマに実施されたキャンペーンの事例を幅広く紹介。様々なキャンペーンを通して、コミュニケーションを成功させるヒントを探ります。

Reaching the target market a limited budget: how is cost effective promotion achieved? What are the most effective ways to combine print and digital media? What expression reaches the target market? The answers lie in this book, with "new ways and forms of communicating with the consumer" as its concept.

948

PICTGRAM & ICON GRAPHICS 2

ピクトグラム＆アイコングラフィックス 2

Page: 208 (Full Color)　¥13,000+Tax

本書では、視覚化に成功した国内・海外のピクトグラムとアイコンを紹介します。空港・鉄道・病院・デパート・動物園といった施設の案内サインとして使用されているピクトグラムやマップ・フロアガイドをはじめ、雑誌やカタログの中で使用されているアイコンなど、身近なグラフィックまでを業種別に掲載。巻末に、一般的によく使われるピクトグラム（トイレ・エスカレーター・駐車場など）の種類別一覧表を収録。

Second volume of the best-seller title "Pictogram and Icon Graphics". Full-loaded with the latest pictograms around the world. Signage, floor guides and maps in airport, railway, hospital, department store, zoo and many more. Contained a wide variety of icons, including those found in catalogs and magazines, etc.

935

WORLD CALENDAR DESIGN

ワールドカレンダーデザイン

Page: 224 (Full Color)　¥9,800+Tax

本書では国内外のクリエーターから集めたカレンダーを特集します。優れたグラフィックスが楽しめるスタンダードなタイプから、形状のユニークなもの、仕掛けのあるものなど、形状別にカテゴリーに分けて紹介します。カレンダー制作のデザインソースとしてはもちろん、ユニークな作品を通じて、様々なグラフィックスに活かせるアイデアが実感できる内容です。

The newest and most distinctive calendars from designers around the world. The collection features a variety of calendar types highly selected from numerous outstanding works ranging from standard wall calendars to unique pieces in form and design, including lift-the flap calendar, 3D calendar, pencil calendar and more.

949

カタログ・新刊のご案内について

総合カタログ、新刊案内をご希望の方は、はさみ込みのアンケートはがきをご返送いただくか、下記ピエ・ブックスへご連絡下さい。

CATALOGS and INFORMATION ON NEW PUBLICATIONS

If you would like to receive a free copy of our general catalog or details of our new publications, please fill out the enclosed postcard and return it to us by mail or fax.

CATALOGUES ET INFORMATIONS SUR LES NOUVELLES PUBLICATIONS

Si vous désirez recevoir un exemplaire gratuit de notre catalogue généralou des détails sur nos nouvelles publication. veuillez compléter la carte réponse incluse et nous la retourner par courrierou par fax.

CATALOGE und INFORMATIONEN ÜBER NEUE TITLE

Wenn Sie unseren Gesamtkatalog oder Detailinformationen über unsere neuen Titel wünschen.fullen Sie bitte die beigefügte Postkarte aus und schicken Sie sie uns per Post oder Fax.

ピエ・ブックス

〒170-0005　東京都豊島区南大塚2-32-4
TEL: 03-5395-4811　FAX: 03-5395-4812
www.piebooks.com

PIE BOOKS

2-32-4 Minami-Otsuka Toshima-ku Tokyo 170-0005 JAPAN
TEL：+81-3-5395-4811 FAX：+81-3-5395-4812
www.piebooks.com